Heave

✦ *101 Glimpses of God's Love* ✦

Can a mother forget the baby at her breast and have no compassion on the child she has borne? Though she may forget, I will not forget you! See, I have engraved you on the palms of my hands.

ISAIAH 49:15-16

Heaven in Our Hearts

♦ *101 Glimpses of God's Love* ♦

Edited by Paul C. Brownlow

Brownlow

Brownlow Publishing Company, Inc.

*H*ow calmly may we
commit ourselves to the hands
of Him who bears up the world.

JEAN PAUL RICHTER

EASELETTES

A delightful miniature product
that will be a big addition to any home
or office because of its small size.
Containing 101 encouraging
quotations, each Easelette will make
a perfect gift or a great way to add
a stimulating thought to your own day.

The person who has a firm trust in the
Supreme Being is powerful in his power,
wise by his wisdom,
happy by his happiness.

JOSEPH ADDISON

EASELETTES

Bouquet of Blessings • Dear Teacher

From Heart to Heart

Home Is Where You Hang Your Memories

Little Bits of Wisdom • On Wings of Angels

Promises for the Journey

Refresh My Heart • Words of Friendship

Heaven in Our Hearts

Thoughts for My Secret Pal

From the Heart of a Friend

Don't try to hold God's hand;
let Him hold yours.
Let Him do the holding
and you the trusting.

HAMMER WILLIAM WEBB-PEPLOE

Every morning lean thine arms awhile
Upon the window sill of heaven
And gaze upon thy Lord.
Then, with the vision in thy heart,
Turn strong to meet thy day.

AUTHOR UNKNOWN

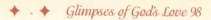

Man may dismiss compassion
from his heart,
but God never will.

WILLIAM COWPER

God is great, and therefore
He will be sought: He is good,
and therefore He will be found.

AUTHOR UNKNOWN

Now thank we all our God,
With heart and hand and voices
Who wondrous things hath done,
In whom His world rejoices.

CATHERINE WINKWORTH

We live today with the everlasting arms
beneath us; we breathe, we eat, we walk,
we think and dream, all because we are sustained
by a universe greater than ourselves and
preserved by a love beyond our fathoming.

JOSHUA LIEBMAN

Earth's crammed with heaven,

And every common bush afire with God.

And only he who sees takes off his shoes,

The rest sit round and pluck blackberries.

ELIZABETH BARRETT BROWNING

Fear not, for I have redeemed you; I have summoned you by name; you are mine. When you pass through the waters, I will be with you; and when…you walk through the fire, you will not be burned. For I am the Lord, your God.

ISAIAH 43:1-3

God loves us
the way we are, but
He loves us too much
to leave us that way.

LEIGHTON FORD

God has a purpose for my life. No other person can take my place. It isn't a big place, to be sure, but for years I have been molded in a peculiar way to fill a peculiar niche in the world's work.

CHARLES STELZLE

Take thine own way with me, dear Lord,
Thou canst not otherwise than bless;
I launch me forth upon a sea
Of boundless love and tenderness.

JEAN SOPHIA PIGOT

God has a thousand ways
Where I can see not one;
When all my means have reached their end
Then His have just begun.

ESTHER GUYOT

The angel of the Lord encamps
around those who fear him,
and he delivers them.
Taste and see that the Lord is good;
blessed is the man who takes refuge in him.

PSALM 34:7-8

*H*ow great a God we need;
and how much greater is our God
than our greatest need.

AUTHOR UNKNOWN

Who hath God hath all;
who hath Him not,
hath less than nothing.

ANCIENT PROVERB

The Lord is gracious
and compassionate,
slow to anger and rich in love.
The Lord is good to all;
he has compassion on all he has made.
The Lord is faithful to all his promises
and loving toward all he has made.

Psalm 145:8, 9, 13

What I have today I have because of His mercy. I did not earn it. I do not deserve it. I did not pay for it. I have no rights to it. I cannot keep it except for one thing—God's mercy.

DAVID CROSBY

*H*eaven will be inherited
by every person who has
heaven in his soul.

HENRY WARD BEECHER

*B*ack of the loaf is the snowy flour,
And back of the flour the mill;
And back of the mill is the wheat,
and the shower, and the sun,
and the Father's will.

MALTBIE D. BABCOCK

I have lived, and seen
God's hand thro a life time,
and all was for best.

ROBERT BROWNING

If the blind put their hand in God's
they find their way more surely than those
who see but have not faith or purpose.

HELEN KELLER

Our ground of hope is that
God does not weary of mankind.

RALPH W. SOCKMAN

The truth about man is that
he needs to be loved the most
when he deserves it the least.
Only God can fulfill this
incredible need. Only God can
provide a love so deep
it saves from the depths.

I can see how it might be possible for a man to look down upon the earth and be an atheist, but I cannot conceive how he could look up into the heavens and say there is no God.

ABRAHAM LINCOLN

*N*ot to us, O Lord,
not to us but to your name be the glory,
because of your love and faithfulness.

PSALM 115:1

*T*he King of love my Shepherd is,
Whose goodness faileth never;
I nothing lack if I am His
And He is mine forever.

SIR HENRY WILLIAM BAKER

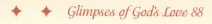

Love is more than
a characteristic of God;
it is His character.

ANONYMOUS

As sure as ever God puts
His children in the furnace,
He will be in the furnace with them.

CHARLES H. SPURGEON

God may not prevent tragedy,
but He enables us
to move beyond it.

KENNETH GIBBLE

O LORD, you are my God;
I will exalt you and praise your name,
for in perfect faithfulness
you have done marvelous things,
things planned long ago.

ISAIAH 25:1

The Lord will rescue me from every
evil attack and will bring me
safely to his heavenly kingdom.
To him be glory for ever and ever.

2 TIMOTHY 4:18

Many favors which God gives us ravel out for want of hemming through our thankfulness; for, though prayer purchases blessings, giving praise keeps the quiet possession of them.

THOMAS FULLER

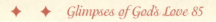
*T*he world is charged
with the grandeur of God.

GERALD MANLEY HOPKINS

The love of God
is no mere sentimental feeling,
it is redemptive power.

CHARLES MORRISON

O love that wilt not let me go,
I rest my weary soul in Thee;
I give Thee back the life I owe,
That in thine ocean depths its flow
May richer, fuller be.

GEORGE MATHESON

✦ ✦ ✦ ✦

*T*here is no need to plead that the love of God
shall fill our heart as though he were unwilling
to fill us. He is willing as light is willing to flood
a room that is opened to its brightness.
Cease to resist, and instantly love takes possession.

AMY CARMICHAEL

God is no fault-finder, always looking
for things to condemn in us.
He estimates us at our best, not our worst.

ANONYMOUS

Happiness is neither within us only,
or without us;
it is the union of ourselves
with God.

BLAISE PASCAL

Praise be to the Lord,

to God our Savior,

who daily bears

our burdens.

PSALM 68:19

Goodness is love in action,
love with its hand to the plow,
love with the burden on its back,
love following his footsteps who
went about continually doing good.

JAMES HAMILTON

*H*ave you ever taken your fears to God,
got the horizons of Eternity about them,
looked at them in the light of His love and grace?

ROBERT J. McCRACKEN

Now thank we all our God
With heart and hand and voices
Who wondrous things hath done,
In whom His world rejoices.

CATHERINE WINKWORTH

I looked at God
and He looked at me,
and we were one forever.

CHARLES H. SPURGEON

Give thanks to the LORD for his unfailing love
and his wonderful deeds for men,
for he satisfies the thirsty
and fills the hungry with good things.

PSALM 107:8-9

*B*ut you are a chosen people, a royal priesthood,
a holy nation, a people belonging to God, that
you may declare the praises of him who called
you out of darkness into his wonderful light.

1 PETER 2:9

A little girl repeating the
twenty-third psalm said it this way:
"The Lord is my shepherd and
that's all I want."

ANONYMOUS

So let it be in God's own might
We gird us for the coming fight,
And, strong in Him whose cause is ours
In conflict with unholy powers,
We grasp the weapons He has given,—
The Light and Truth, and Love of Heaven.

JOHN GREENLEAF WHITTIER

God is he without whom
one cannot live.

LEO TOLSTOY

He who has no friend
has God.

EGYPTIAN PROVERB

Some people complain because
God puts thorns on roses,
while others praise Him
for putting roses among thorns.

ANONYMOUS

I have never committed
the least matter to God,
that I have not had reason
for infinite praise.

ANNA SHIPTON

Just as there comes a warm sunbeam
into every cottage window,
so comes a love-beam of God's care
and pity for every separate need.

NATHANIEL HAWTHORNE

◆ ◆ *Glimpses of God's Love 23* ◆ ◆

I never made a sacrifice.
We ought not to talk of "sacrifice" when
we remember the great sacrifice
which He made who left His Father's
throne on high to give Himself for us.

DAVID LIVINGSTONE

For God so loved the world that he gave
his one and only Son, that whoever
believes in him shall not perish
but have eternal life.

JOHN 3:16

This thought shall cheer me:
That thou art near me,
Whose ear to hear me,
Is still inclined.

ANONYMOUS

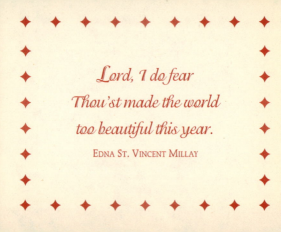

Lord, I do fear
Thou'st made the world
too beautiful this year.

EDNA ST. VINCENT MILLAY

How great is the love
the Father has lavished on us,
that we should be called
the children of God!
And that is what we are!

1 JOHN 3:1

The light of God surrounds me
The love of God enfolds me
The power of God protects me
The presence of God watches over me.
Wherever I am, God is.

ANONYMOUS

You may trust the Lord too little,
but you can never trust
Him too much.

ANONYMOUS

*H*uman beings must be known
to be loved, but divine things
must be loved to be known.

BLAISE PASCAL

God is not in the slightest degree baffled or bewildered by what baffles and bewilders us. He is either a present help or He is not much help at all.

J. B. PHILLIPS

A man can no more diminish God's glory by refusing to worship Him than a lunatic can put out the sun by scribbling the word "darkness" on the walls of his cell.

C. S. LEWIS

God has revealed many truths which He has not explained. We will just have to be content to let Him know some things we do not and take Him at His word.

B. A. COPASS

How often we look upon God as our last and feeblest resource! We go to him because we have nowhere else to go and then we learn that the storms of life have driven us, not upon the rocks, but into the desired haven.

GEORGE MACDONALD

It is not because things are good that we are to thank the Lord, but because He is good. We are not wise enough to judge as to things, whether they are really joys or sorrows. But we always know the Lord is good, and everything He provides or permits must be good.

HANNAH WHITALL SMITH

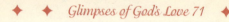

I would rather walk with
God in the dark than go
alone in the light.

MARY GARDINER BRAINARD

Who reaps the grain and plows the sod
Must feel a kinship with his God:
For there's so much on earth to see
That marks the hand of Deity.

ROBERT W. STUART

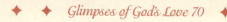

*D*elight yourself in the Lord
and he will give you the
desires of your heart.

PSALM 37:4

*G*od's gifts put man's
best dreams to shame.

ELIZABETH BARRETT BROWNING

*E*ach of us may be sure that if
God sends us on stony paths,
He will not send us out on any journey
for which He does not equip us well.

A<small>NONYMOUS</small>

The love of God is one of the great realities of the universe, a pillar upon which the hope of the world rests. But it is a personal, intimate thing too. God does not love populations, He loves people. He loves not masses, but men.

A. W. TOZER

Silence

I need not shout my faith.
Thrice eloquent are quiet trees
and the green listening sod;
Hushed are the stars,
whose power is never spent;
The hills are mute:
yet how they speak of God!

CHARLES HANSON TOWNE

Dear Lord and Father of mankind,
Forgive our foolish ways!
Reclothe us in our rightful mind,
In purer lives Thy service find,
In deeper reverence praise.

JOHN GREENLEAF WHITTIER

Love is the greatest thing that God can give us,
for himself is love; and it is the greatest thing
we can give to God, for it will also give ourselves,
and carry with it all that is ours.

JEREMY TAYLOR

I will proclaim the name of the Lord.
Oh, praise the greatness of our God!
He is the Rock, his works are perfect,
and all his ways are just.

DEUTERONOMY 32:3-4

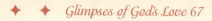

Never be afraid to trust
an unknown future to
an all-knowing God.
CORRIE TEN BOOM

God loves each one of us as if there were only one of us.

SAINT AUGUSTINE

The LORD will guide you always;
he will satisfy your needs
in a sun-scorched land
and will strengthen your frame.
You will be like a well-watered garden,
like a spring whose waters never fail.

ISAIAH 58:11

Take comfort, and recollect however little
you and I may know, God knows;
He knows Himself and
you and me and all things;
and His mercy is over all His works.

CHARLES KINGSLEY

*I*f Christ lives in us, controlling our personalities,
we will leave glorious marks on the lives we
touch. Not because of our heavenly characters,
but because of His.

EUGENIA PRICE

Glorious indeed is the world of God
around us, but more glorious the
world of God within us.

HENRY WADSWORTH LONGFELLOW

Dear friends, since God so loved us, we also ought to love one another. No one has ever seen God; but if we love one another, God lives in us and his love is made complete in us.

1 JOHN 4:11-12

You, dear children, are from God and have overcome them, because the one who is in you is greater than the one who is in the world.

1 JOHN 4:4

There is nothing you can do to make God love you more! There is nothing you can do to make God love you less! His love is unconditional, impartial, everlasting, infinite, perfect! God is love!

ANONYMOUS

God does not love us because
we are valuable.
We are valuable because
God loves us.

FULTON J. SHEEN

*G*od is a light that is never darkened;
an unwearied life that cannot die;
a fountain always flowing;
a garden of life; a seminary of wisdom;
a radical beginning of all goodness.

FRANCIS QUARLES

Life passes, riches fly away, popularity is fickle,
the senses decay, the world changes.
One alone is true to us;
One alone can be all things to us;
One alone can supply our need.

JOHN HENRY NEWMAN

Praise be to the God and Father of our Lord Jesus Christ! In his great mercy he has given us new birth into a living hope through the resurrection of Jesus Christ from the dead, and into an inheritance that can never perish, spoil or fade — kept in heaven for you.

1 PETER 1:3-4

It is but right that our hearts
should be on God,
when the heart of God
is so much on us.

RICHARD BAXTER

Those who attempt to search into
the majesty of God will be
overwhelmed with its glory.

THOMAS À KEMPIS

You have made known to me the path of life;
you will fill me with joy in your presence,
with eternal pleasures at your right hand.

PSALM 16:11

This, this is the God we adore,
Our faithful, unchangeable friend,
Whose love is as great as his power,
And neither knows measure nor end.

JOSEPH HART

God's love for poor sinners
is very wonderful,
but God's patience
with ill-natured saints
is a deeper mystery.

HENRY DRUMMOND

We sometimes fear to bring our troubles to God, because they must seem so small to him who sitteth on the circle of the earth. But if they are large enough to vex and endanger our welfare, they are large enough to touch his heart of love.

R. A. TORREY

None but God can satisfy the
longings of an immortal soul;
that as the heart was made for Him,
so He only can fill it.

RICHARD TRENCH

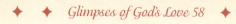

Give God thy broken heart,
He whole will make it.

EDMUND PRESTWICK

Nature is too thin a screen;
the glory of the omnipresent God
bursts through everywhere.

RALPH WALDO EMERSON

*P*raise be to the God and Father of our Lord Jesus Christ, the Father of compassion and the God of all comfort, who comforts us in all our troubles, so that we can comfort those in any trouble with the comfort we ourselves have received from God.

2 CORINTHIANS 1:3-4

If we have got the true love of God shed
abroad in our hearts, we will show it in our lives.
We will not have to go up and down the
earth proclaiming it. We will show it in
everything we say or do.

DWIGHT LYMAN MOODY

One of the many pleasures of old age
is to become ever more sharply aware
of the many mercies and blessings
God showers upon us.

MALCOLM MUGGERIDGE

*H*is divine power has given us everything we need for life and godliness through our knowledge of him who called us by his own glory and goodness. Through these he has given us his very great and precious promises.

2 PETER 1:3-4

Measure not God's love and favor by
your own feeling. The sun shines as clearly
in the darkest day as it does in the brightest.
The difference is not in the sun,
but in some clouds.

RICHARD SIBBS

It is impossible for that person
to despair who remembers that
his Helper is omnipotent.

JEREMY TAYLOR

He paints the lily of the field,
Perfumes each lily bell;
If he so loves the little flowers,
I know he loves me well.

MARIA STRAUS

Oh the sheer joy of it!
Living with Thee,
God of the universe,
Lord of a tree.
Maker of mountains,
Lover of me.

RALPH CUSHMAN

*O*ur only warrant for believing that God cares is that he has communicated this fact to us. It is the key fact about himself which he has chosen to reveal to us, and it is the most comforting fact imaginable.

LOUIS CASSELS

Know that the LORD is God. It is he who made us,
and we are his; we are his people,
the sheep of his pasture.
Enter his gates with thanksgiving
and his courts with praise.

PSALM 100:3-4

*G*ratitude is not only the memory
but the homage of the heart—
rendered to God for his goodness.

NATHANIEL PARKER WILLIS

God brings no man
into the conflicts of life
to desert him.
Every man has
a Friend in Heaven
whose resources are unlimited.

MORRIS

God is our refuge and strength,
an ever-present help in trouble.
Therefore we will not fear,
though the earth give way
and the mountains fall into
the heart of the sea.

PSALM 46:1-2

*O*pen your eyes
and the whole world
is full of God.

JAKOB BÖHME

How Thou canst think so well of us,
And be the God Thou art,
Is darkness to my intellect,
But sunshine to my heart.

ANONYMOUS

With God in charge of our defenses,
there will be peace within.

T. T. FAICHNEY

Be not afraid in misfortune.
When God causes a tree to be
hewn down, He takes care that
His birds can nestle on another.

ANONYMOUS

Be absolutely certain that our Lord loves you, devotedly and individually, loves you just as you are.... Accustom yourself to the wonderful thought that God loves you with a tenderness, a generosity, and an intimacy that surpasses all your dreams.

ABBE HENRI DE TOURVILLE

He tends his flock like a shepherd:
He gathers the lambs in his arms
and carries them close to his heart;
he gently leads those
that have young.

ISAIAH 40:11